Rianna Webster

A New Reality and One Year Without You

AUSTIN MACAULEY PUBLISHERS™
LONDON • CAMBRIDGE • NEW YORK • SHARJAH

Copyright © Rianna Webster 2021

The right of Rianna Webster to be identified as author of this work has been asserted by the author in accordance with section 77 and 78 of the Copyright, Designs and Patents Act 1988.

All rights reserved. No part of this publication may be reproduced, stored in a retrieval system, or transmitted in any form or by any means, electronic, mechanical, photocopying, recording, or otherwise, without the prior permission of the publishers.

Any person who commits any unauthorised act in relation to this publication may be liable to criminal prosecution and civil claims for damages.

All of the events in this memoir are true to the best of author's memory. The views expressed in this memoir are solely those of the author.

A CIP catalogue record for this title is available from the British Library.

ISBN 9781528946582 (Paperback)
ISBN 9781528971836 (ePub e-book)

www.austinmacauley.com

First Published 2021
Austin Macauley Publishers Ltd®
1 Canada Square
Canary Wharf
London
E14 5AA

Table of Contents

Nan	6
Chapter 1: Just Another Day	10
Chapter 2: Never Give up Hope	18
Chapter 3: Third Time Lucky	22
Chapter 4: Freedom	29
Chapter 5: Nan's Birthday	32
Chapter 6: The Calm Before the Storm	34
Chapter 7: The Day Heaven Gained an Angel	39
Chapter 8: The Hardest Day	45
Chapter 9: The First Visit	47
Chapter 10: A Sign from God	51
Chapter 11: Goodbye My Angel	55
Chapter 12: Making Sense of It All	60
Chapter 13: Homecoming	62

Chapter 14: A New Beginning	64
Chapter 15: Alone with My Thoughts	67
Chapter 16: The First Christmas	69
Chapter 17: The Opening of the Ashes	72
Chapter 18: A Rose for Each Generation	74
Chapter 19: Another Year Older	78
Chapter 20: Nan's Birthday	80
Chapter 21: Mothering Sunday	82
Chapter 22: Eleven Months an Angel	84
Chapter 23: One Year Without You	87

born in 1944. Grandad was in the British Army having joined up at the age of 15 and served his duties during the World War II. During the time he was away, Nan was pregnant with Helen (Granny). Imagine that? Being pregnant during the war and may well even be thinking, 'What if my husband doesn't come home?' Nan's youngest daughter was born towards the end of the war.

Sadly in 1982, Nan and Grandad were separated upon his death, leaving Nan widowed. Nan remained true and faithful to Grandad; she never met anyone else nor did she have any desire to, either. I guess you could say that certainly vows back then really were for life. When you married someone, you stayed true to them and even when times were tough, you fought it out as a couple, which doesn't seem to be the case in this day and age.

While he was alive and they were together, Nan and Grandad spent some time living on a boat as they both loved sailing. They belonged to a sailing club when in 1988, Nan became the first woman to become rear commodore, and in 1990, Nan became vice commodore.

In 1964, Nan became a first-time grandmother. Nan's eldest daughter, Helen, gave birth to a daughter named Natasha, who is the mother to Jake and I.

Despite being four generations apart, our family were very close. We still are very close, but in particular I felt like Nan and I had a close relationship.

Growing up, Jake and I probably only ever saw Nan once or twice a week. I can't quite remember exactly how often but quite regularly. I remember one time, my Nan knitted me this cardigan, it was white and it had clear buttons knitted into it. It was beautiful. As well as being clever, Nan was also quite creative, always knitting or sewing – a very talented lady. One year at Christmas time, instead of buying an advent calendar for Jake and I, Nan made us one with pockets on it with the numbers on which he has sewed on, and each morning there would be a little present inside the pockets, like a small toy or a chocolate. Thinking back on it, I wish I still had it, but I can't remember where it is.

When my brother and I were young, unfortunately our parents separated and Nan allowed Mum, Jake and I to live with her for a couple of years until Mum could get a place for the three of us to live. However, during the time that the three of us were living with Nan, there were a few arguments therefore my Granny (Helen), stepped in and spoke to Mum, saying that Mum, Jake and I could go and live in her flat which she had previously rented out.

By not living with Nan, I feel that it actually brought us closer as we were not seeing her and were not under her feet every day. I can't explain why Nan and I were close. We just had a close relationship, maybe it was something to do with being a great granddaughter.

When Jake and I were little, sometimes when Nan came round, we would play catch. Now that could have been with anything, a soft ball, a bean bag or even sometimes, a smelly old pair of socks, and whenever it was my turn, Nan would always point her finger and use one of her most famous catchphrases, "Watch the ball," and even till this day, whenever I have to catch something, those words run through my head. Another game that we used to play with Nan was called 'Find the Thimble'. This game was always really funny, because Nan used to love sewing; she always had thimbles about. The rules were very simple: Jake and I would have to close our eyes and wait for Nan to hide the thimble and then we would have to find it. It's as easy as that.

As well as playing catch, Nan had a love for card games, which may have rubbed off on me a little because whenever we went round to see Nan, we would always find time to play a card game. She taught me loads of games from Snap to Rumi, and of course the famous 52-card pickup.

On the subject of just how close we all were, being four generations of woman, it made us even closer. Poor Jake, having to deal with all us women on his own, that was until Mum met Neil, which was a really good thing as it meant that there was another man that could sympathise with Jake.

In 1998, Nan made the big decision to move from Teddington, London to Redhill, Surrey to be closer to the family. It didn't take her long to think about it; as soon as she saw the house, she fell in love it. It's funny though because the house that Nan did eventually buy, it wasn't actually her first choice. Nan got the house because the agent who was dealing with her first choice wasn't being very helpful, so she told them where to go and went with someone else who helped her buy the place that she lived in, and Nan really enjoyed her time in Redhill. She had a beautiful garden, and she had all her family around her. Nan had a wonderful 18 years in her house and never once did she regret the move.

Chapter 1
Just Another Day

Just to introduce myself to you all, I'm Rianna, without the 'h', and I'm just a typical 20-year-old student studying Access to Nursing at East Surrey College, Redhill, Surrey, and at around 5 o'clock this evening on my way back from college, I got a phone call from my mum asking me where I was. I thought it was a bit strange that Mum was asking me this question as she never usually rings me on a college day. This made me think that something wasn't right. I replied to Mum's question saying, "I'm walking home from college. I'm literally two minutes away from home." I asked Mum what's wrong. She didn't sound right on the phone and what Mum was about to tell me, I wasn't mentally prepared for.

Mum said to me that Nan had been rushed to hospital and that Neil (my stepdad) was on his way home to pick me up. I dropped my phone in shock. I quickly picked my phone up off the ground and then continued my conversation with Mum. I said to Mum, "Sorry, I dropped my phone. Okay, see you in a bit." As soon as I hung up, I instantly rang Mum back; being in such a state of shock, I forgot to ask Mum what actually had happened to Nan. Mum told me that Nan had suffered a stroke but the doctors had said that it was only minor and not to worry. I quickly rushed home and waited for Neil to pick me up.

I have always had a close relationship with my Nan. We're a pretty close family, we go out for meals and family days out. There is something so special about knowing your great grandparents. It's one thing to know your grandparents, but for me to say that I know my great grandmother, that is something special and something of a privilege.

Before I knew it, Neil arrived home and picked me up, and drove us both to East Surrey Hospital as that's where Nan had been taken into. Despite the hospital being only 10 minutes away, the journey felt like an eternity. When we finally got to the hospital and saw Nan, my heart sank. There she was, looking so frail and vulnerable. This was something that I had never seen in Nan before. Nan had always been this strong, independent woman. She would do anything for any of us. Nan always put us before herself and now here she was, in hospital fighting to recover. I felt so helpless. I just wanted to take it all away but I couldn't, because there wasn't anything that I could do. The only thing that I could do in that moment was to hold Nan's hand, letting her know that I was there, providing some kind of reassurance that all will be okay even though I didn't know what the future will be. We all stayed by Nan's side for a while longer but time was getting on and visiting hours were coming to an end, even though I didn't want to leave, I had no choice. I reluctantly said my goodbyes to Nan and told her I love her, and that I will see her tomorrow.

It's been a while since I've been home from seeing Nan and at this moment in time, I have so many thoughts going through my head. I don't think I have actually registered anything that I have just seen. Did I really see what I thought I saw? Is this some horrible nightmare that I'm going to wake up from? I can't stop worrying about Nan. I knew time must have been getting on a bit so I checked the time, 11:30pm, and I have college tomorrow so I better try and get some sleep.

So, it's now 07:15am, my alarm has just gone off and quite frankly, I don't understand why I set my alarm this early because I never get up straight away – I have about four different snooze alarms. But on this particular occasion, I can't go back to sleep. I'll be honest and say that I didn't get a lot of sleep last night. Yesterday's events are running through my head. I was sort of hoping that it was all a nightmare and that I am going to wake up from it but in my mind, I know that it isn't going to go away. I'm sitting on the end of my bed debating whether to go to college today or do I call up and say I'm not coming in. After a moment of thinking about it, I've decided that it's probably best that I do go to college as I need some distraction from what's currently going on.

Once I'm ready for college, I have to double-check I've got everything, such as college ID, keys, purse, phone, the usual things that most people do before they leave home. I say a quick goodbye to Mum and give her a kiss on the cheek like I always do and leave the house. As I'm walking to college, I still can't control my thoughts, it's like my head just keeps replaying the same thing over and over again like a broken record.

So, college started roughly about half an hour ago and I'm sitting here at a laptop looking at a blank page. I've been staring at this screen for over half an hour and I've not typed a single word. I just can't focus. No matter how hard I try, my mind just doesn't want to co-operate. I did genuinely think though that by coming in today it would keep my mind distracted and I will forget about last night; however, this clearly hasn't worked as the only thing that I can seem to think about are my thoughts and feelings.

Since I have arrived at college this morning, a few people have asked me if I am okay. Because I don't want to talk to anyone about what's actually happened, all I can say to people is, "Yeah, I'm fine." my reasons for not wanting to tell anyone are simply based on the fact that if I talk about it, then it becomes real and I don't want it to become real, however, I know I have to talk to my teacher because I need to talk to someone. It's just finding that right time when she's not busy with other students and I can tell her then.

It's now lunch time. I've lasted half a day so far at college and it's doing my head in; most days college does my head in, so it isn't unusual for me to say that. However, these feelings are more intense. I know I need to leave college and get out of here because I feel like I'm just wasting my time, going nowhere and achieving nothing. I mean, so far in the whole day, I have probably only written about four lines, that's it. It's pointless me being here today.

Just before our lunch break came to an end, I spot my tutor so I walk over and talk to her. I told her what had happened, that my Nan is in hospital and I'm struggling to concentrate at college due to everything, and I can't focus on anything else. My only thought is, I want Nan to be okay. My tutor is surprisingly nice about it all, as she is allowing me to leave early. I pack up all my belongings and leave college. I went home and later on that evening, I went to hospital to see Nan. When I arrived at the hospital and I saw Nan for the second time; in that moment, it all hit me. This isn't a nightmare, this is real. My eyes started to well up with tears as I knew that my Nan wasn't going to be the same person that she always had been. This was the start of a new reality.

As the days have passed by, in my head I've been thinking "I must tell Jake." He's my brother, so I must tell him. I have to let him know that Nan is in hospital. Now the reason my brother doesn't know yet is because at this moment in time, Jake doesn't live at home. He's in the army and is currently at where he is based, which isn't too far away from home. However, Mum has told me not to tell him as he is away and she doesn't want to worry him. I respected what Mum was saying so I haven't said anything. However, a few days have passed since I had that conversation with Mum, and I can't keep it from him any longer. I need to let Jake know, I don't care if Jake isn't home, he needs to know that Nan is in hospital because I know if it was me and I was away from home then I would want to know what was happening. I picked up my phone and rang Jake's number. Jake didn't answer straight away and I didn't want to leave a message saying what had happened. I simply left a message saying, "Hi Jake, please can you ring me back when you get this message as it is important." Within minutes, Jake got back to me. I spoke to him and told him what had happened. I said that I was sorry for not calling sooner. Thankfully, Jake wasn't mad, he understood Mum's reasoning for not wanting to tell him straight away but he appreciated that I had told him. We chatted on the phone for a bit longer; Jake said that he would be down at the weekend like he usually was and that I would see him then.

A few weeks have passed by and Nan is beginning to show small signs of improvement; however not as much as we would like. Unfortunately, Nan can no longer verbally communicate. We can see Nan's trying to speak but sadly no words are coming out. Can you imagine how Nan must be feeling, imagine yourself, just for one second that you couldn't speak. The frustration must be unreal. Speech is something that is taught from such a young age that you do it without thinking about it. It's the main form of communication and when that gets taken away so suddenly, you have to figure out an alternative method of communicating. We have tried to encourage Nan to write, however that wasn't working very well so we tried using a letterboard so Nan could spell out what she wanted, however that didn't appear to be working either. The speech and language therapist team so far have been really good. They are still continuing to work with Nan as I'm writing this. However, it's not all been bad. Nan is finally able to eat and drink again. She's recognising who we all are and remembers how we are related to her. Nan's son-in-law put together a photo album soon after Nan fell ill. Inside the album had photos of all of us with our names underneath and in brackets the relation to Nan. For example, underneath the photo of me it says Rianna (Great Granddaughter), or a photo of Mum it says Natasha (Granddaughter). I think this has definitely contributed to Nan being able to recognise who we are to her.

At this moment in time, Nan has spent a duration of two and a half months in hospital. And today is the day that Nan is finally able to come home. Nan spent five weeks in East

Surrey Hospital and five weeks in Crawley Hospital for rehabilitation. The hospital is about a 20-minute drive from where we all live. It was amazing to see Nan in her own home. She seems to be happy to be back in her own environment. Nan is able to walk around her house. She is now using a Zimmer frame to keep her balance but even so, seeing Nan walking again is something that I didn't think I would see again. I can't thank the hospital enough for the treatment that they gave to Nan, not only were they looking after Nan but they were supportive of us as a family. Seeing someone you love in hospital is never easy. As a carer myself, when you're looking after someone, you sort of become part of their family too. You're there to support and take care of the patient but you're also there supporting the family. Watching Nan come through the front door of her house, you could see that she recognised exactly where she was. My Nan was finally home.

You can tell that Nan is happy to be home. Let me just describe to you what Nan's house looks like. It's quite a modern style house. As you walk through the front door, on the right is the living room which has the dining room backed onto it. The kitchen is on the left of the dining room. At the back of the house is a conservatory which Nan had extended when Jake and I were younger. To the left of the front door is a downstairs bathroom. The staircase on the left, and upstairs there are two bedrooms, one spare room and another bathroom. The house also has a front and back garden which Nan takes great pride in. Not only is the house lovely but it is in a prime location, right in the centre of town.

During the time Nan had been in hospital, we didn't make any adjustments to her house, we wanted to see how she would cope in her home with the layout continuing with how it looked before Nan was rushed into hospital, so as it's the first night, we haven't done anything. We're just going to see how it all goes.

Today is day two of Nan being home and yesterday evening was just a trial run to see how she is coping at home. It has become apparent that it isn't safe for the house to stay as it is. Mum rang Neil and asked him if he could come round to help move some things around the house. We all felt that it isn't safe for things to stay as they are and as a family we have this fear that "What if Nan gets up in the night?"..."What if she falls down the stairs?" So many things. We have now converted the dining room into Nan's bedroom. By doing this, it means that when we all come round to see Nan then there's plenty of room for all of us to sit and Nan can still be included in conversation. It also makes transferring from wheelchair to bed easier as there is no need to go upstairs. Another bonus is that Nan can look out in the garden. However, the most important reason that we have made all these adjustments is that Nan can still live at home and be in her own environment, which she has always been used too.

Chapter 2
Never Give up Hope

It has been about 10 weeks since Nan came out of hospital, and she is doing really well. Since she has been at home, Granny has moved in to be with Nan to help look after her; essentially, Granny has become Nan's primary carer. We have recently started to use carers twice a day from a care company. I won't say their name, but I can't fault them; they have been so good with Nan. They come round twice a day like most care companies, once in the morning and then again in the evening. Another positive is that the majority of the carers are genuinely really nice people. I say majority because there has been the occasional one that I haven't been particularly keen on but most of them are okay. I think it's just human nature to not take to everyone, although the world would be a much better place if everyone liked everyone else.

So, for a while now, things have been starting to settle down at home. We've all got used to a new routine, carers coming in at the same time most days, and things are sort of starting to calm down a bit, which has been really good. It's meant that I have been able to focus a bit more on my studies.

We are in the middle of June now and I am coming towards the end of my Access to Nursing qualification and what a year it has been. Despite the struggles that have gone on this past academic year, I have really enjoyed my course. Before starting this course, I had just completed my Health and Social Care National Diploma. My aim is that, hopefully, once I complete this qualification then I can continue my studies and become a nurse. However, I might take a year out of education then go back to it later.

There have been a few times during my studies when I could have just walked away and not looked back at all. There were times when I just didn't want to go to college and could have quite happily stayed at home. However, growing up I have always been told to never give up. You just got to push on through the hard times because the end result will be worth it. I have had a great deal of support from my tutors. They've all been really good and without that support, then I probably wouldn't have been able to come as far as I have done, and in just a few short weeks from now, I will be collecting my certificate which, hopefully, will be good news.

A few weeks have passed by and today is the day that I am going to college to collect my certificate. Let me tell you now I am absolutely petrified, even though I know it's going to be good news. Well, I don't, but I know that if I tell myself then it makes it easier to deal with. I put my headphones on as I make my way to college. During this time I am reflecting on this past year. This year certainly hasn't been the easiest but I feel that with everything that I have been through, I might have somewhat grown up a bit; my view on life has changed completely. Never take anything or anyone for granted because in a few short hours, everything could be different. I started to think back to when I started my course back in September 2012. When I told Nan that I wanted to study this Nursing course, she said to me, "Rianna, you will make an excellent nurse someday." Nan helped me pay for my course; being over 19 you have to pay for further education. I think subconsciously that has been a big reason as to why I didn't want to give up. By giving up I wouldn't just be letting myself down, but I would be letting my family down, I would be letting Nan down.

Before I knew it, I was at the college gate ready to collect my certificate. It's in a hard-backed envelope and I'm just about to open it. Part of me is really excited to see what it says, however, there's another part of me that is still nervous. It's strange because I don't even know why I'm scared as I know what is inside this envelope. After I had completely opened it, I gently took out my certificate and had a look at it. Despite how difficult this year has been, I have achieved a merit as my final grade and I am very proud of myself. My classmates are all planning to go out and celebrate, however I'm on my way to Nan's house. I want to show her just how well I have done.

I've just got to Nan's house and she is in the front room, watching TV. As I walk into the front room, she turns her head towards me then looks down at envelope that is in my hand. Nan then looks at me with smile on her face. I thought it would be funny to tell Nan that I had failed my course and in my hand was a failure certificate. So that's exactly what I'm doing, however she knows I'm lying. I smile back at Nan and hand over my certificate for her to look at. I can see Nan's looking at it carefully, really taking in every word that is on the paper. She hands it back to me with a smile on her face and pats me on the head. That's her way of telling me that she is really proud of me and I know that she fully understands what she has just read.

Chapter 3
Third Time Lucky

So, it has been a year since Nan has come home out of hospital. As I mentioned earlier, we have engaged a care company and still to this day we have continued to use them. However, alongside them we began using a live-in care company. When we first started using them, they were really good; a carer would come and live with Nan for one week a month, then the rest of the month we would go back to using carers twice daily. This meant that Granny could have a break from being with Nan all the time. Now don't get me wrong, Granny has never complained about looking after Nan, however, being a carer myself, it can get mentally and physically draining, and it did Granny a lot of good to be able to go back to her place to get some proper rest. By using this live-in care company one week a month, has allowed Granny to have some time to herself and has made looking after Nan a lot easier.

We only used the live-in care for about eight to nine months. It was really good to start with but after a while we realised that actually it wasn't working and no longer wished to use them. So for the past four months, we have reverted back to using carers morning and evening, however, as a family, we make sure that Granny does still get her break and for one week a month where previously we would have used live-in care, Mum will go round and help look after Nan. Sometimes I go round on days when I don't have to go to work the following day.

About six months have gone by since we stopped using live-in care, so Nan has been home for the past 18 months. We are currently in late June and during the past few months, I have had a change in career. I now work in a nursery in Woodhatch. I haven't been there long, probably two, maybe three months. So far I'm really enjoying it, the staff are friendly, which you would expect with it being a nursery. The age group of children that I work with are two-and-a-half to three-year-olds. They're at that age where they can back chat you, but because they are sweet you can't stay mad. I know this feeling all too well as my baby brother is about the same age. Not only are the staff friendly but the manager here is really supportive. Even though I'm working more days, the hours are shorter and I have a set shift pattern. Here it's Monday–Friday, but at the care home my days varied each week. This made it more difficult for me to arrange some sort of social life. Whereas now, I have a set shift pattern which makes going out and enjoying my social life a lot easier.

July 18th 2014, today is the day that I am about to take my driving test. Now I've already tried taking my test twice already and I've failed both times. First time was because some idiot thought it was acceptable to step out in the middle of the road without even looking; of course I emergency braked, however because the examiner felt the need to touch the brake pedal on his side, it became an instant failure.

Second attempt I'm not even going to go into as it's not even worth telling; however, let's just say I had the same examiner as I did on my first attempt. I'm just hoping and praying that I don't have him today, otherwise I think I'll give up the idea of driving all together. However, there is this famous saying known as "third time lucky". Let's hope this applies to me today. Now at this moment in time, I'm waiting to be picked up by my driving instructor, who funnily enough, has the same name as my work manager. She's been so good with me, putting up with all of my frustrated outbursts or my mental breakdowns halfway through a lesson because I've been struggling with something. A very lovely lady. As the clock ticks and time goes by, my nerves are becoming more apparent. I'm almost regretting my decision to take my test. Before I know it, I receive a text from my instructor saying that she's outside. In my head I'm thinking, "This is it, there's no going back now. Next time I'm home, I would have either passed or failed."

The time is now 10:45. I've just had an hour's driving lesson before my test, which is scheduled for 11:00, so I've got nothing to do but wait until my name is called. Honestly, this feels like the longest 15 minutes of my life. I'm looking down at my phone replying to a few people who have messaged me saying that, "I hope your test goes well,", "let me know how it all goes," and before I knew it, 11:00 came, my name was called and my test has begun. As I'm driving, I have this feeling that I'm going to pass my test; I don't know why, I just have this really good feeling about it. I know this sounds quite big-headed, but at the moment I'm doing well, and at the moment there doesn't seem to be any reason for me to not pass. Before I knew it, I was back at the driving centre. It was in this moment that I was going to be told if I failed or if I passed. My driving examiner looked at me with a smile on her face and she said to me, "Rianna, I am pleased to tell you that you have passed your driving test." I put my arms around her and gave her a hug, and without thinking about it I shout at the top of my lungs, "About bloody time!" I can feel my eyes welling up with happiness. I turn my head to look at the driver next to me. I knew he hadn't passed; he had this look of sadness on his face. I feel a bit bad for him because I know what it's like to be told you failed. I handed over my provisional driving licence, and she gave me my certificate. Before she left, she said to me, "You're driving licence should arrive within the next two to three weeks, however, in the meantime, you can use this certificate as proof that you are a qualified driver. Congratulations once again." I replied "Thank you" and with that she got out of the car and went back to the test centre.

I turned my head to look at the back of the car where my driving instructor was sitting, as I was allowed to bring her with me for support. She wasn't allowed to intervene or say anything during my test, but she knew I had passed before I knew it. I said to her, "Did you know I had passed?" She smiled at me and said, "I had a feeling you had. Well done, Rianna." She got out of the back and got into the passenger side of the car. I told my manager at work that I had my driving test today. She had allowed me to have the day off, which I think is pretty decent of her. She had asked me to keep her updated on what happens, so I feel like I have to drive to work and tell her the good news. I asked her if I could pop into work to tell my manager that I passed my driver's test. She agreed, so we made our way over to my work place.

I walked into work and went to the manager's office, which is right next to the door as you walk in. She looked up at me and asked me, "What happened?" I looked at her all sad-faced. She had the 'oh god' look on her face. I smiled and showed her my certificate. " I passed!" She smiled at me and gave me a hug, then looked at me and said, "Congratulations." I asked her if I could have a pay rise so I could buy a car. She laughed and said to me, quite bluntly, "Nice try, but no." Fair enough, I couldn't argue with that. After a few minutes, I had to say goodbye and make my way back to the car as my instructor had learners to teach. I got back into the car and drove back to where I live. A strange feeling came over me, I'm not too sure how to describe it. It's like a happy feeling but at the same, kind of a sad one. Saying goodbye to my instructor feels quite difficult. It's been a long journey but I finally got there. I looked at her and gave her a massive hug, thanking her for putting up with me, for dealing with me when I've had a bit of a meltdown, when I've felt like giving up, but most importantly, for getting me through my test. She said to me, "It's been a pleasure to teach you, best of luck with your driving and once again, well done to you." With a smile, I left and ran upstairs to ring my mum, granny and nan to tell them the news.

    I dialled Mum's number first and told her that I had passed my driving test. She sounded absolutely thrilled to hear that. After while of chatting on the phone, I dialled Nan's number. Granny picked up the phone as she is living with Nan. I told Granny that I had passed my driving test. She was ecstatic, over the moon. Granny told me that she still remembered the day that she passed her driving test. It's a feeling that you never forget, the happiness that you feel when you get told that you've passed is unforgettable. I politely asked Granny to put me on the phone to Nan. I said hi to Nan, then I told her the news. Now even though I know that Nan cannot verbally communicate, she made this excited sounding noise, as if that was her way of congratulating me. I can tell from how she sounds that she's happy for me. I spoke to Nan for a bit longer and then she passed the phone back over to Granny. I told Granny that I was on my way over as I wanted to show them both my driving test certificate.

I put my shoes back on and grabbed my house keys and made my way over to Nan's house. When I arrived, I rang the doorbell. Granny answered the door and gave me a hug. I hugged her back then walked in to the front room. Nan just looked at me and gave me this smile that just lights the room. I walked over to her, wrapped my arms around her and gave her a kiss on the cheek. I knelt down beside her and handed her my certificate. She looked at it, not just a quick glance, she really looked at it, taking in every word and really understanding what it was that she was reading. After Nan had finished looking at it, she looked back at me, smiled and gently patted me on the head. I said to Nan, "If you and Granny hadn't paid for me to have my first set of driving lessons, then I wouldn't be here right now showing you my driving test certificate. Thank you, Nan. I love you." Nan just laughs, she always laughs when people say to her that they love her, I think it's adorable.

A few hours have gone by, and I decide that it's time for me to make a move. I needed to go into town and buy a couple of bits before the shops close and then I'll go home. I said my goodbyes to Nan and Granny, and walked into town. Nan only lives a two-minute walk away. All I needed to get was the basic female necessities. "Oh, the joys of being a woman," I thought to myself. Once I got all that I needed, I made my way home. It didn't take me long to get home as I also only live just up the road from town. We're quite lucky like that as a family. We all live near each other, and we're quite a close family. Being four generations of women, we form a unit. And Nan by far definitely wears the tiara. She is the queen of the family.

Chapter 4
Freedom

It's been two months since I passed my driving test, and today is the day that I am getting my first car. I don't know what I want and if I'm honest, I'm not particularly bothered, as long as it has four wheels, I don't mind. Granny mentioned a place called Three Arch Garage, that's where Jake got his first car from, and I'd heard some good things about that place, so Mum, Granny and I went down to have a look at the cars that they have there. Even though I didn't really know what I was looking for, I had some determination to buy a car today. To be able to walk away with a car of my own would be amazing.

When we arrived, I was just casually looking, and test-drove a couple of cars but none of them really took my fancy. However, Granny spotted this navy-blue Volkswagen Polo, 2005 plate, manual – it looked lovely. I asked the salesman if I could test-drive it. He agreed and as we got in the car, I fell in love with it. I turned the engine on and went for a little drive. As soon as we got back, I knew straight away that it was the car I wanted. Granny offered to help me pay for it and get all the paper work sorted. As soon as all that was done, he handed me the car key and that was it. I thought to myself,

"It's official, I have my first car." Mum got into the passenger side and sat with me as I drove the car home. I think I was getting a bit too confident as when we got the end of the road, I stalled. I started laughing, but that really put me in my place. Mum told me not to worry, it was a new car and it was normal to stall sometimes. After a moment, I managed to get the car moving again. Mum and I are just having general chit-chat conversation, and before I knew it, we were home. Mum looked at and gave me a hug. She said to me, "Well done, my darling, I'm so proud of you." I said to mum that he needs a name. Mum said to me, "Oh, he's a boy, is he?"

"Yeah, I think I'll call him Kevin." We both laughed at my choice of name for him, but to me, he looks like a Kevin.

As soon as I parked up outside my house, I remembered that it was the summer BBQ at my previous workplace. I told Mum that I am going to pay my previous workplace a visit for the BBQ, to which she replied, "That's okay, however, please let me know when you are there." I gave her a kiss and a cuddle goodbye. Before driving, nerves started to kick in at the thought that this was going to be my first time driving a car alone. Even though I know I can drive, it's still daunting the thought of driving by myself. However, driving alone is something that I will have to end up doing at some point, so I may as well do it now and get used to it. I turned the car engine on and began driving. My previous workplace is only about a five-minute drive, however it feels longer when you're slightly nervous. Before I knew it, I had arrived and pulled into the car park. The car park is full up, so my only other alternative is to park in the main road; sooner or later, I found a parking spot and turned the engine off. I sent Mum a quick text message to let her know that I got here okay, to which she was best pleased about. It felt nice to be back; even though I'm only visiting, there's something nice about being in familiar surroundings. I bumped into a few of the residents that I used to care for, which was quite nice, having a good old conversation with them. On the whole, it was quite a nice afternoon, seeing everyone again and having a nice little catch-up with people.

Chapter 5
Nan's Birthday

February 15th 2016: today is Nan's 94th birthday, and I am getting ready to go see her. Even though it's a Monday and I should be at work, I managed to get it off, so I could be a part of Nan's special day. 94 is such an amazing age to get to; despite all the health struggles that Nan has been through, she's a real fighter and got through it. Maybe that's her generation; what people of Nan's age went through growing up has made them into fighters, it's their way of life. Nan was born in 1922, so she's been through a lot during her life so far, which meant that she went through The Great Depression of the 1930s and World War II.

I made my way over to Nan's house to celebrate her birthday. Now even though Nan only lives a five-minute walk away from where I live, I decided to drive over to Nan's house. Now that's not me being lazy, that is for valid reasons, such as taking a cake round, not just any old cake, it's a chocolate cake, and it's not just any old chocolate cake, it's a Rianna special – in simple terms, I made it.

I've just arrived at Nan's house and the house is full of people. Obviously, Granny is there, but I'm talking about a couple of people that I haven't seen in a long time. Nan's cousin is here and an old family friend as well. The pair of them are lovely people. You wouldn't think Nan and her cousin are related, as they are two completely different sort of characters. Nan's cousin is very outgoing, very confident, she won't beat around the bush, she'll just say it as it is and doesn't really care. A bit of a wild one, whereas Nan wasn't as confident, she used to worry about things, she wouldn't voice her opinion, she was always the peacemaker. So, it was always exciting when Nan's cousin came round.

We decided that we were going to watch the horseracing on TV, so that we could all bet on the horses. We all put 50p in the middle of the table, which is also known as a kitty, and whoever's horse won, they would get the money that was in the kitty. Just as I was starting to run out of change, one of my horses finally got their arse into gear and won a race. However, the overall winner of the day is definitely Nan. She's always been lucky with things like this, even though she has never been a gambler. When she does make a bet, she usually wins it, same with whenever she goes to a raffle fair, or even playing a simple game of cards. I guess you could say that on the whole, Nan is quite a lucky person.

Now the racing has finished, Granny and I are getting Nan's birthday cake ready to take in so that Nan can blow out her birthday candles. We didn't put 94 candles on the top, for two reasons, one being that blowing out 94 candles will be quite the challenge, and two, there isn't enough room for 94 candles. Although next year, we may have to try it out, which means that we would need to get a bigger cake.

Chapter 6
The Calm Before the Storm

Friday 26th August 2016: today is a really nice day today. The sun is shining and surprisingly, the weather is really hot outside. This type of weather is a rare occurrence for Britain. Most of the time the weather can be quite misleading; it looks sunny but when you go outside, it's like stepping into a freezer. Another bonus is that I happen to be off work today, so what better way to spend the day than seeing my beautiful Nan. Due to my shifts this week, I haven't been able to go round and see her as much as I would have liked too. As soon as I arrive at Nan's, I am pleased to see that Nan is looking rather well. She's a lot more alert than she has been the past couple of days, so it's nice to see her on a good day. Maybe it's the hot weather, I know I always feel better on a hot day.

I say hello to my auntie and uncle, who were there as they have been staying with Nan for the past week or so as they live quite a distance away. I grab a chair and place it at the side of Nan's bed and hold her hand to let her know that I'm here. After a moment, my auntie walks in and I ask her if she knew when they next planned to come and visit. She replies, "Probably in about a month or so."

I looked at Nan and told her that I was going to go outside in the garden for a bit, just to enjoy the hot weather whilst we still had it.

As I sit here in the garden, I soak up the sun, listening to the birds twittering away, having their own little conversation. It actually put a smile on my face. I would love to know what they were saying to each other. I am also thinking about what am I going to do with the rest of my day. I'm working all weekend so I won't have much time to do anything, so whilst I have the day off, I better try and get some things done. I'm also going out later with a friend of mine, so I need to plan my day wisely. A little while later, I make my way back inside to sit with Nan. Zoe, my best friend, is on her way over to pay Nan a visit before we head out. It wasn't long from the time she messaged me to say she was on her way over to when she actually arrived. She brought Nan a packet of Kit Kats as she loves them. I took one out of the packet to give to Nan and put the rest in the fridge due to the hot weather, as I didn't want them to melt.

As I sit here with Nan, watching a bit of TV, a thought comes to me, which is I'll make Nan a Kit Kat sundae on Monday as that is my next day off. In fact, after the weekend, I'm off until Wednesday, so I get a good few days with Nan. I decide to leave it until Monday because at this moment in time, Nan is starting to become tired, or she certainly looks tired; however, because she's had a pretty good day today, I'm hoping that Nan will be just as good on Monday when I next see her.

I glance at the clock across the room and notice that time is getting on a bit. I have a few things to do before my friend and I head out for the evening and because Nan is tired, I think it's best that I say my goodbyes to Nan now to allow her to get some proper rest. I lean over and softly speak into Nan's ear, "Okay, Nan, I'm going to make a move now. I'm actually working tomorrow and Sunday, so I won't be round until Monday. However, I'll make sure to give Granny a call tomorrow to see how you are. I love you, Nan, you get some rest and I'll see you Monday." I hold her hand and give her a gentle kiss on her head before I leave the room and head towards the front door. I turned my head towards Nan. As I'm looking at Nan, this awful feeling comes over me. A thought in my mind is telling me that my time with Nan isn't as long as I think, Nan's time is limited. I don't dare tell anyone what I am feeling as it's probably me being silly. With that, I quickly dismiss that thought and leave the room to crack on with my day.

Chapter 7
The Day Heaven Gained an Angel

Saturday 27th August 2016: I was getting ready to go to work. I checked my phone casually to see what the time was only to realise that I had a missed call from Mum. Just as I was about to call her back, Jake walked into my bedroom with tear filled eyes. I looked at him and I had this horrible feeling that I already knew exactly what he was going to say, I just did not want to believe it. Jake told me, "Nan has passed away." I didn't say anything. All I could do was cry. I heard Jake walking towards me; he gave me a hug and after a moment I realised that I had to call up work and tell them that I wasn't going in that day and that I wouldn't be in the day after.

After I had phoned up work, I put my shoes on, didn't even change out of my work uniform. I just grabbed my car keys ready to go. Jake took the keys out of my hand and chucked them on the bed. He looked at me and said, "No, neither of us are in a fit state to drive, we are walking." I just nodded. I knew he was right and we both began to make our way to Nan's house. As we were walking, I felt like I was in a dreamlike state, like nothing felt real. It was only yesterday when I saw her and she seemed fine.

As we approached Nan's house, I felt sick. Jake knocked on the door and Granny answered it. For a split second, I hesitated. I didn't want to go in. I knew that I had to, as I needed to see it for myself. As I walked in to Nan's house, the first thing I noticed was soft music coming from the front room, which had become Nan's bedroom. I gave Granny a hug then I walked into the front room and gave Mum and Neil a hug. After that I turned to face Nan's bed and there she lay, eyes shut, looking more peaceful than she had looked in a long time. With tear filled eyes, I grabbed a chair and put it to the side of Nan's bed, reached out and held her hand. Her skin was still warm, and this meant that Nan had not long passed away.

After a while of sitting next to Nan, holding her hand, I went to stroke her face. It was cold, that sort of cold that you can't describe, but it sends chills through your spine. I instantly flinched away in shock, and it was in that moment that I knew Nan was gone. When I went back to touch her hand, it was warm. I knew in that moment that it was my body heat keeping her hand warm and without me realising it, her whole body was gradually cooling down.

I sat with Nan a little longer, but I knew I needed to get some air, so I went outside and as soon as the fresh air hit my lungs, I felt sick. I started coughing and heaving, thinking that I was going to be sick but nothing came up. Just as I was recovering from my coughing episode, I saw a white butterfly fly pass right by me and a weird feeling came over me. It felt like Nan was sending me a sign, like it was her letting me know that she was okay.

I went back inside and Granny had just come off the phone to her brother-in-law who Granny had been trying to contact all morning but every time she rang there was no answer. I noticed that Granny was very frustrated after talking to him; who wouldn't be, he was an arrogant man. He had been shouting at Granny because Granny's sister had found out Nan had passed away through an email from one of Nan's neighbours. I certainly wasn't best pleased to hear that so I went round to Nan's neighbours house and spoke to her in a calm but firm tone of voice.

I knocked on her door and respectfully said, "Excuse me, can I have a word with you for a moment?" Her reply was "Yes, come in." I stopped for a moment, just thinking about what I was going to say. I couldn't risk my mouth getting the better of me so once I knew exactly what to say, I went inside her house and spoke to her. I started off by saying, "Just before I start saying what I want to say, I'm not here to cause any trouble but as you are aware, my Nan, your neighbour, has sadly passed away this morning and to my knowledge I understand that you have e-mailed my great auntie and told her that you were sorry to hear of Nan's passing. However, with all due respect, I don't believe you had any right to do so. We have been trying to contact them all morning to tell them the sad news and when we do finally get through to them, Granny gets an earful from that brother-in-law of hers saying that you emailed them. You know, put it this way, Granny's sister has just found out that her mother has passed away through an email that you sent. Can you imagine what she must be feeling? We still have family members that are yet to be told, I appreciate that you sent your condolences and that you thought you were being kind, but at this moment in time, while it's all still so raw, it would be appreciated if you or no one else that isn't family got involved"

After our little chat was finished, I walked back to Nan's house to be with the family. During the time that I had been away, Granny had rung the doctors and informed them that Nan had passed away. We needed to have a doctor come round to verify her death. I went outside and rang up Zoe, who is my best friend. She didn't answer her mobile so I rang her landline. In my head I was thinking, "Come on, please pick up." As soon as there was a "hello" at the other end of the phone, I was relieved to know it was her who had answered the call. I said "Zoe."

She knows that it's me. She said "Rianna, what's wrong?" I couldn't say anything, all I could do was cry. Zoe continued the conversation by saying, "What is it?" Judging by her tone of voice, I think she knows what I'm going to say as she sounds really sad on the other end.

After a minute, I manage to say, "It's Nan, she's gone. Nan has passed away."

I can hear her voice cracking on the other end of the phone as she's talking to me. At this point, Nan's other neighbour came outside and asked, "What's wrong?" Whilst Zoe was on the phone, I told her what had happened. She gave me a hug and told me, "I'm so sorry for your loss, things do get better though, I know it doesn't feel that way at the moment but things will be okay."

The doctor turned up. I told Nan's neighbour that I have to go now, completely forgetting that Zoe is still on the phone. I said to Zoe, "I'm sorry but I have to go now, the doctor has just arrived."

She said, "Okay, I'll come round later if you want me to."

I said, "Yeah, please."

Zoe replied, "Bye, sweetie." I hung up the phone and went inside.

When I went back into the house, the doctor got out her stethoscope and explained to us that she had to listen to her chest to see if there were any light sounding heartbeats or some sort of sound. Now in the back of my head, I was thinking my nan has passed away, she isn't breathing, there isn't going to be a heartbeat of any sort. I was beginning to feel slightly angry, but I didn't interfere, I just allowed the doctor to do what she had to do. When the doctor had finished doing her checks, she confirmed Nan's death. The doctor recommended that we should call the funeral home and get the undertakers to collect Nan's body as soon as possible due to the weather being hot outside. As a carer myself, working in a care home, I have had experience with death before losing my Nan, and whenever we lost a resident, to a degree I guess you do feel some grief for that person as you knew them, you looked after them and nothing is the same. But when you lose a family member, the whole grieving process is entirely different and all those negative feelings are so much more intense because you have genuine love for that person.

After the doctor had left, Granny and I went outside. She lights up a cigarette, and I have one with her. We stay outside for a few moments afterwards, just talking about how things will be so different without Nan, but that we will get through it as a family, because that's what we always have done. We get through things together. A few more moments pass by and we decide that now is the time to call the funeral home.

After we ring the funeral home, Granny said to me, "Rianna, take Nan's wedding ring, she would want you to have it." I said no at first. In my head I thought to myself, "That's Nan's wedding ring, I can't take it. It's not right." Just before the undertakers arrived, I have a change of heart. I decided to take Nan's wedding ring and placed it on my finger. It fits perfectly.

When the undertakers arrive, all Granny, Mum, Jake and I can do is watch as they wrap her in a sheet. They place her delicate body onto the stretcher and place that dreadful black bag over her body before they carry her to the car. We all follow behind and watch as they gently place her body in the back of the car. We watched them drive off, taking her body to the funeral home. Little did I know that the image of seeing what I had just witnessed would keep re-playing in my head, keeping me awake at night and constantly give me nightmares.

After the car drove away and was out of sight, Mum, Granny, Jake and I go back inside, and being a carer, I unintentionally went into work mode. I unplug the air mattress and wipe it down properly with the anti-bacterial wipes. I stay at Nan's house a while longer before I make my way home. Shortly after arriving home, Zoe came round. She said that she would stay the night. I think she knows that I wouldn't sleep much if I was by myself.

Chapter 8
The Hardest Day

Some people say that the hardest day is on the day that you lose someone you love, but for me, I think that the hardest day is the day after, because this is the start of a new beginning. It's learning how to cope with new situation, and it started right from when I woke up this morning. Yesterday was such a blur that I can't remember it, not fully. There are bits to it that I remember very clearly; the one thing that stuck in my mind and has kept me awake all night has been when the undertakers came and took my Nan's body away, I think that has left me with some sort of post-traumatic stress disorder because I had a real vivid nightmare of that last night. Every time I went to sleep, this is what I saw. When I woke up this morning, I felt an emptiness that only my Nan could fill, and it feels stronger today than it did yesterday. Maybe because I know that I won't ever be able to go round there and see her again, maybe because all of this is becoming all too real for me to deal with and accept.

Yesterday's emotions were full of shock the day after, so today is when all the memories come back to you. And for me, every emotion is running through my head. I feel sad, I feel angry, I feel guilty. There were times when I could have gone round and didn't. There were times when I probably could have done more and didn't. If I'm being totally honest with you, I don't really know what I feel. I have so many emotions all at once that all I feel is numb. I can't pinpoint on a certain emotion because they're all combined together.

As well as feeling all these emotions, you start to think to yourself: What do I do? How do I cope without Nan? Why me? Why my family? Why my Nan? And as all these thoughts are going through my head, I can feel all the unwanted anger burning up inside me like a volcano, ready to explode any second. But the worse part of feeling all this anger is that there is nothing to take it out on. There is no one to shout at, no one to blame, because it isn't anybody's fault.

Chapter 9
The First Visit

The weekend of Nan's passing fell on a bank holiday. This meant that the funeral home wasn't allowing any visitors until Tuesday (30th August 2016). I did go and visit Nan, however due to my shift pattern at work, I wasn't able to go until the Saturday (3rd September 2016). I remember asking my friend if she would come with me. I didn't want to go by myself. I knew I couldn't face going by myself, but what I did know is that I wanted to see her again. It still hadn't fully sunk in that Nan had left us.

Saturday morning arrived faster than I wanted as I wasn't sure if I was ready or how I would cope. Zoe picked me up and drove us to the funeral home where Nan was. As Zoe parked the car, I felt sick. My eyes were filling with tears and my heart was racing a million miles an hour. After a moment of calming down, we both got out of the car and started walking towards the main reception. I pressed the bell and this kind gentleman let Zoe and I in. I told the man that I was here to see my Nan, Beryl Pettitt. The man showed Zoe and I the waiting area and told us to wait there for a few moments and that he would come back when it was okay for me to go in.

A few moments went by, and what must have only been about two minutes, felt like an eternity by the time the man came back. He said to me that I was allowed to go and see Nan now, and he led me to her room. My eyes started to well up. I asked him if I could have a few minutes before entering. He looked at me and replied, "Take all the time that you need, there's no rush." A thought went through my head that it must be quite difficult for the undertakers to prepare a body for viewing. They don't know this person, they have no personal attachment, yet they do their best to make them look like they are sleeping rather than deceased.

After a few minutes, I finally grabbed the courage to walk in, and what I saw, nothing could have prepared me for. I saw Nan's coffin with the lid removed. I quietly walked towards her, not really knowing what I was about to see. I looked inside and there Nan was, just lying there in a beautiful coffin. She was wearing a beautiful black dress with a light green vine pattern printed on to it, dotted around with beautiful white flowers. She looked stunning. In fact, the dress that she was wearing was the same one that she wore at her 90th birthday party. However, when I looked at her face, I couldn't recognise her. The way they had stitched her mouth closed. It was scary, almost Joker like. It was very un-natural. I ran out of the room as fast as lightning to grab my friend. I needed her with me to go back and see Nan because even though I knew that it was my Nan, it scared me not being able to recognise her.

Zoe came running over as soon as I called her and she gave me a hug as I just stood there. She asked me, "What happened?"

I just stood there and said, "It doesn't look like her, I can't recognise my Nan." Zoe asked me if I wanted to leave, but I said no. I needed to go back in.

Together, we walked back towards Nan's room and as we walked in, the sensor-linked air freshener went off. I thought my Nan was breathing. I asked Zoe if she heard that. "Heard what?" she replied, and when I told her what it sounded like, she must have thought I was going mad, but I was convinced that Nan was breathing. The sun was shining through the gaps between the blinds. The window was slightly open so the cool breeze blowing through the blinds made it look like her chest was rising. That same noise happened again, this time Zoe heard it and she told me that it was just the air freshener.

It was in that moment that I knew I had to leave. My mind was messing with my head and I knew I needed to get out of the room. I couldn't recognise my Nan, I thought I heard her breathing, I thought her chest was rising, and it was all these thoughts put together that freaked me out. I told Zoe that I'm going to sit with Nan and say my goodbyes and then we can leave. I grabbed the chair that was provided in the room, placed it at the side of Nan, sat down and reached out to hold her hand and said my goodbyes to Nan. Before I left the room, I gently stroked her face and ran my hand through her hair whilst I softly kissed her head and I whispered into her ear with tear-filled eyes, "I love you, Nan. Until we meet again, you sleep tight, my angel." After that, I left the room and shut the door behind me. Just before leaving, I kissed the tips of my fingers and gently touched Nan's door.

I did go back to see her again, one last time. I knew that it wasn't healthy to keep going to see Nan the way she looked. I knew that I had to start accepting and find some way of coping with the reality of what was going on. And what was going on was that it didn't matter how many times I went back to see Nan, she wasn't coming home. She's made her new home up in heaven with other angels as her neighbours. What I do know is that my Nan is with me wherever I go because I think about her every day. There's a saying I once heard which goes like this, and it's one that my friend Joe told me, "A person is never truly gone until there is no one left to think about them." Everywhere you go, you'll always see a sign from an angel above, letting you know that they are watching over you. You may hear a song on the radio, or you may smell a certain scent. If you open up your mind and look a little harder, then you'll start to recognise them.

Chapter 10
A Sign from God

Nan never really spoke about what she wanted at her funeral. After all, who wants to talk about what happens to them when they pass away. However, because of this, as a family, we didn't really know what Nan would have wanted. Would Nan have wanted to go to church the night before her funeral? Or would she have wanted to go from her home? We didn't know. So, what we did was to incorporate the two. Nan remained in the funeral home from the 27th August to 21st September.

On the afternoon of 21st September, Mum, Granny, Jake and I got a taxi from Granny's home to the funeral home where we waited for our Nan to appear in the funeral car. I went outside the gates to clear my head and then I saw her. I saw the undertakers wheel the coffin over the car and gently lift her into the back of the car. I looked over to Mum, Granny and Jake, and I drew their attention by pointing towards the car, to which they all came over to where I was and we all just watched as they drove the car up to where we were all standing.

Mum, Granny, Jake and I walked back over to the taxi and made our way to the church. We asked for the car to stop outside Nan's house for a couple of minutes. That way, it was like Nan was going from her own home and not from the funeral home. After a few moments, we continued to make our way to the church where Nan would stay overnight before her funeral the following day.

We had a bit of a troublesome drive to the church as some idiot thought it would be acceptable to cut us up at a set of traffic lights, meaning that now there was the funeral car, this idiot and then the car we were in. I got really angry that another car was behind Nan and not us, so of course anyone that knew me would know instantly how I would react. After a few moments of shouting and saying the occasional rude word to the driver in front, I think he finally got the hint and moved out of the way.

When we got to the church, we asked how much the fare was and we expected it to be much more than what he charged, considering he had to wait about 30 minutes at the funeral home and stop outside Nan's house. But the kind taxi driver didn't charge us waiting time. He was very respectful to us and generous with his price. As I got out of the car, I apologised for my foul language. He just smiled and said, "Don't worry about it, I've heard worse. Hope it all goes okay tomorrow." We gave the driver a tip before he drove off and thanked him for his kind service.

Jake got out the taxi first and he walked over to the funeral car as he was helping to carry Nan into the church. We all watched as Jake and the undertakers got Nan out of the car, gently lifted her up onto their shoulders and carried her into the church. As they began to make their way into the church, we all followed behind her and took our seats where a short service took place. It was difficult for me to accept that my Nan was in that coffin, let alone how Jake must have felt, as he was carrying her into the church. Sometimes I wonder how the undertakers manage to cope with it.

Once the service had finished, Mum, Jake, Granny and I lit a candle at the front of the church in memory of Nan. As we were all leaving the church, Francis, who is the church reverend, came over with some lovely words. Her words were, "Never in all my years of being involved in the church, have I ever seen all the colours from the stained-glass windows and the rays of sunlight shine on the walls so brightly. It looked beautiful, that's a sign from God, letting you know that your Nan is okay and that she is safe with him."

I took great comfort in those words, however, I found it very hard to leave the church that evening, knowing that the following day we would all be saying our final goodbyes to a lady that brought so much joy to us as a family, and did so much for everyone. That beautiful lady was my Nan.

After we left the church that evening, the four of us went out for a meal and had a drink for Nan. I guess you could say this was the first stage in the family pulling together and getting used to the new reality of life without Nan. It's moments like this where you really do start to appreciate the people that you have around you because sooner or later the day will come when they won't be. Although it felt strange going out for dinner without Nan being there, it wasn't all that depressing. We were sitting there talking about the memories that we had with Nan and reliving the past times.

There were a few funny moments during the night so I would say that on the whole it was relatively quite a nice evening.

Just before leaving, Granny did her typical, "I'm going out for a fag." I did go out and join her for one. The two of us were sitting on the benches outside in the pub garden and we were just having general chit-chat about how the day has been. We were talking about that even though this next year would be hard, as it would be the first full year with her, together as a family we will pull through because that's something that we have always done and will continue to do so.

After a while or so – I don't think either of us was timing how long we'd been outside – we went back inside to pay the bill and got a taxi back home. When I got home, I looked at my phone and noticed that a couple of people had messaged me asking how the day went. I replied back saying that it went okay and if they were free that evening, could we all meet up and go out for a drink, to which they said yeah. A couple hours later, my friend came round to pick me up as she knew I would not be in a good state of mind to drive. We went to a social club where we met another friend. The three of us went inside and had a drink for Nan. It was my idea to go out because I thought that the longer I was out, the less time I would be thinking about tomorrow. What I completely forgot when I suggested where we met was that the club was right behind the church that my Nan was. Just before we left the club, I looked over and through the darkness of the trees, I could see the silhouette of the church against the sky and without me knowing, my eyes had started to fill. I had held them back all day and then suddenly they all came out and I didn't know how to stop them.

Chapter 11
Goodbye My Angel

22nd September 2016: The big day, the day that we have all been dreading but knew would come. Today is the day that we all say our final goodbye to a lady that was very special to everyone. She was a mother, a grandmother and a great grandmother. She was the queen of the family, the lady that you would go to if you ever needed advice or if you didn't know what a word meant then she would be able to tell you instantly what that meaning was. Nan was one of the most amazing women that I had the privilege to know and I felt so lucky and so proud to be her great granddaughter.

Mum, Jake, Neil, Zoe and I went to Granny's house in the morning, as the funeral car was picking us up from Granny's house to take us to the church. It was a bit of a stressful morning. I was nervous about doing a reading for Nan. I wanted it to be perfect and I was so scared I wouldn't do it justice. Granny was stressing out about whether the car was going to be here on time and the whole morning was a bit hectic. However, when the car turned up and we were actually on our way to the church, things sort of calmed down a bit. When we got to the church, we all waited outside for everyone to take their seats.

A few people came over to us to say hello before going inside and once everyone had gone in to take their seats, Granny, Mum, Jake, Neil, Zoe and I walked in and sat down in the pews that was reserved for family. I looked around the church and noticed that my great auntie and uncle along with their daughter were not sitting in the family section, they were near the back of the church, almost as if they didn't want to feel part of the family. It bothered me slightly because even though there has always been friction between Granny and her sister, today wasn't about that, it was about celebrating the life of a wonderful lady. I didn't say anything though as it was their choice as to where they sat. However, maybe I could have misinterpreted the whole thing and they just didn't cope well at funerals which is why they had chosen to sit near the back.

As the service started, everyone stood up and we sang Nan's favourite hymn: 'Dear Lord Father of Mankind.' It was after the Gospel reading where we had the family tributes. The vicar started by reading out the eulogy of Nan's life which was written by Granny. Granny found it difficult to read so the vicar stepped in and offered to read it out on her behalf.

Once Granny's piece was finished, Mum and I went to the front of the church to do our reading which we had both prepared. It wasn't so much a piece of writing that we had written but we both read out a lovely poem that we had come across. I asked Mum to go first. She stood there and read out her poem. All of a sudden, it was my turn and I was thinking to myself, "Come on, Rianna, you can do it." I placed my poem on the stand in front of me, took a breath and began reading it. The poem that I had chosen was titled 'He Only Takes the Best' and is as follows:

> *He Only Takes the Best*
> *A heart of gold stopped beating,*
> *Two shining eyes at rest,*
> *God broke our hearts to prove to us, He only takes the best.*
> *God knows you had to leave us,*
> *But you did not go alone,*
> *For part of us went with you, the day He took you home.*
> *To some you're forgotten,*
> *To others just part of the past,*
> *But to those that have loved and lost you,*
> *Your memory will always last.*

After Mum and I had said our poems, we both stood in front of Nan's coffin, facing the church and bowed our heads to Nan as a sign of respect and then returned to our seats.

When the service came to a close, Jake stood up, followed by Neil, and they took their places either side of Nan's coffin. With the help of the undertakers, they gently lifted Nan up onto their shoulders and began to carry her out of the church. The rest of the family stood up and followed out walking behind Nan. Looking around the church, there wasn't a dry eye in sight. Once we had all left the church, the rest of the congregation followed along behind. We watched as they placed Nan into the funeral car and then we got in the funeral car behind Nan, took our seats and made our way to the crematorium. I would say it took about 15 minutes to get to the crematorium from the church. When we arrived and got out the car, Jake and Neil went over to the funeral car where Nan was and once again with the help of the undertakers, they carried Nan into the crematorium. At the crematorium, we had a short service, which quite a few people from the church service also attended. There was a large turnout of family and friends.

We were asked by the funeral director before the service if we would like to have the curtains closed or left opened at the end of the service. We said that we would like to have the curtains remain open as we were leaving. At the end of the service, we had a song playing that Mum chose which I burnt onto a CD. The song that was chosen was 'We'll Meet Again' by Vera Lynn. As the song began to play, we all stood up. Granny, Mum, Jake and I all went over one by one to Nan, gave her one last kiss before leaving the room to the garden where we had arranged for a dove release to be held. Two doves: the meaning behind the dove release was that one of the doves was meant to represent our great granddad and the other dove was there to represent Nan. Jake and I wrote a little message on a Rizla paper which got attached to the foot of each dove. We did a countdown so that way we could release them at the same time. By releasing the doves at the same time, this meant that now Nan and our great granddad could be reunited together again.

After the dove release, we went back over to the funeral car and made our way back to the church where we had the wake. There was food and drink; I was surprised to know that my Granny only had two glasses of wine. She could usually go through half a bottle, although Granny always says that she's only had one glass because she would never let the glass get empty, she would just top it up pretty often.

A few people came over to us as we arrived back to the church and said to us just how wonderful the funeral was. One lovely lady said, "That was the most beautiful funeral that I have ever been to." And she was right, the service went as good as it could have possibly gone. A perfect send-off for a perfect lady.

Chapter 12
Making Sense of It All

A week or so after my Nan's funeral, I found myself at the top of Reigate Hill, which is a popular viewing point. With it being close to the end of September, there was a slight dampness in the air and the leaves were just beginning to start falling from the trees, landing softly on the ground. There were loads of different colours ranging from yellow to brown, some were red, some were a burnt orange sort of colour too. This time of the year shows nature at its most beautiful.

In the solitude of my surroundings, I sat in my car and started to think about previous events, gathering up all of my thoughts, trying to put them together in a way that made sense. I had loads of questions running through my head. Things like, what exactly is life and death? We start off as a tiny new-born baby and as we grow up, we form relationships with people, we go out and have a few laughs, and we shed a few tears. We make a career for ourselves. Some people settle down and have a family. What happens to all of that? None of that stuff matters when you're gone, not really. What about all the knowledge that we learn during our lifetime, where does it all go? What about the relationships that we make during our lifetime, the love that we feel, the experiences that we have when we are alive, where does it go when we pass away?

I don't know how long I was sitting there thinking to myself, but after a while, I noticed the sky looked a bit grey. I thought that I better make a move on my way home before it started to rain. I looked at my phone and saw what the time was. I turned the engine on, switched on the headlights and drove home.

Chapter 13
Homecoming

When it was time to collect Nan's ashes, the whole thing was devastating. Mum, Jake, Granny and I went to the funeral home to collect them. We were asked to wait in the waiting room whilst they went to get her ashes and bring them over to us. It was weird being back at the funeral home as the last time I was there, I was visiting Nan, seeing her body, and now I'm here to collect her remains.

Looking around the waiting room, I could see all these different ornaments, from rings to paper weights. The most fascinating part was that all these ornaments were made from a single teaspoon of ashes. Mum and I were talking and really contemplating about whether we would want to buy one. I thought about getting a ring; Mum thought about either a necklace or possibly a ring too. However, in the end we both decided against it, but the option was still there.

Before we knew it, the gentleman that had showed us to the waiting room appeared with a box; inside that box were Nan's ashes. He handed the box over to Granny and we went over to pay the bill. The total price that we paid included the funeral, the cremation, the funeral car and the collection of the ashes. Whilst Granny was paying the bill, she had tears in her eyes. It was heart-breaking to watch. It's a sight that no grandchild wants to see, let alone what Mum must have been feeling watching her mother cry.

After the bill was paid, we left the funeral home and went back to Granny's house. We placed Nan's ashes under a picture of Nan that we already had hung up on the wall.

Chapter 14
A New Beginning

With Nan home, we felt the time was right to clear out Nan's house and put it on the market. We all went round and put things into certain piles. One pile was full of stuff that needed throwing out, one pile contained things that we decided could go to the charity shop and another pile was full of things that we all wanted to keep. I chose to take Nan's decanters; I don't know why but I have always liked the look of them, they are old-fashioned and very beautiful to look at. I also wanted Nan's bureau, a beautiful piece of furniture. It's almost like a little writing desk that people years ago would have used. To open it, you flip the top down and then either side there are two drawers which you pull out to stabilise it. I can feel Nan's presence when I sit at the writing desk and I imagine her sitting here writing letters with the kind of care that isn't apparent in today's digital world.

After we had a good look through everything and we had chosen what we would like as a memento of Nan, we bagged up the things that were in the charity shop pile and took them down there. As there were a lot of things to take, I said to Granny that I would put a couple of bags in the boot of my car and take them down during the week. When it came to it, I unloaded the bags of items out of my car and carried the bags to the door of the charity shop. The charity shop was closed at the time I went to drop the items off, so I left the bags outside the front door. As I was walking away, I had a change of heart and I couldn't part with it. I wasn't ready. Nan's charity items stayed in my car for a further eight months. After that, I felt like maybe it was time to part with Nan's belongings. It was time for them to be owned by someone else.

It's funny how no one knows how much stuff they actually own until it needs to be cleared out.

Once all of Nan's things were cleared, we put the house on the market and within a few short months, the house was sold. At first, I thought to myself, "I don't want anyone else living there." I wasn't happy with the idea that another family was moving into the property that was part of my life for so many years.

One night when I was at Granny's house, we were watching *Call the Midwife*, a BBC Drama programme which is set in 1950s Britain. Whilst watching this one particular episode, a line in the programme caught my attention and went something along the lines of this: 'The house doesn't hold the memories. The memories go with you as you created those memories.' Suddenly the light bulb in my head went off and it all made sense, that it was time for me to accept and be okay with a new family moving in and creating their own memories, as I had done for the past 18 years of Nan living in Redhill.

Although I was able to accept a new family moving in to Nan's old house, I did keep my original set of Nan's house keys, just as a little reminder of the house. It's a simple keyring with three silver keys on it, each with a different colour nail polish on it so I could tell which key belonged to which door. There's one for the front door, one for the back door and one for the conservatory door. Although the locks they fit are probably long gone, just holding these keys in my hand keeps the connection with Nan and my memories of her.

I did however go back to the house one final time, just before the new family moved in. I got all emotional but I knew that I had to say goodbye to the house. I knew that I would never forgive myself if I didn't go back. First of all, I went upstairs and went inside all of the rooms to have one final look around the room. As I walked out of each room, I shut the door behind me. I then went downstairs and did the same, room by room I walked into each one, had a final look and shut the door behind me, knowing that the next time all these doors get opened, it will be a fresh start for a new family to make their own memories. There were people in the house before Nan brought it and now there's a new family moving in. Houses just sit there as an observer of human life, watching people come and go.

Chapter 15
Alone with My Thoughts

I find myself back at Reigate Hill, thinking about the recent events of disposing Nan's personal property. Reigate Hill is where I tend to do a lot my thinking because it's quiet, which allows me to think clearly. Why am I thinking about it? Well, it was all triggered by driving past Nan's house one day on the way home from a friend's house – part of my normal journey home. However, this time it was different because the new owners were in the house and the lights were on.

I suddenly felt a rush of anger take over my body and it came from nowhere. I thought I had come to terms with a new family being there but it was apparent that subconsciously it was still in the back of my mind. And seeing this new family, inside a house that belonged to my family for so long, it felt like they were invading, intruding or trespassing. I didn't want them there. I just wanted to break into the house and chuck them all out.

I sat at this viewing point for probably about an hour or so, coffee in my hand, watching as the day faded away, saying to myself, "I have to accept that things move on. It isn't healthy to hold on to something that isn't going to change."

It felt like my mind was arguing with itself. One part was saying, "Move on, Rianna," whilst the other part of me was saying, "Hold on to everything you have because once you let go, it's gone forever." My conscious thought was stuck somewhere in between and it is very mentally draining, and as each day goes by, you are waiting for the pain to go away. You wake up some days just wishing it to go, but it doesn't. It becomes easier to deal with, and with each passing day, the pain becomes a little less, but the emptiness that you feel, that never goes away.

However, after a little while, I came to a solution on what is best for me. I realised that the best solution was not to make a decision but to stop overthinking everything and let time do its healing day by day.

crackers, telling those typical cracker jokes that just make you cringe – sometimes you get the odd one that is actually quite funny. And then you always get these little toys that come inside them, plus a paper crown which everyone expects you to wear.

I guess you could say that on the whole, it was a good day. Despite how different the day felt without Nan, she was still part of the day. Perhaps not in body, but in mind.

Chapter 17
The Opening of the Ashes

It's been a couple of months now since we collected Nan's ashes and during these past couple of months, we have been talking about opening the container that they came in. Mum, Granny and I had this miniature urn which we were going to fill with Nan's ashes, only a couple of teaspoons in each urn. We had the idea that we were going to separate Nan's ashes. Some of them were going into the church memorial garden and some of them were going into the River Thames, for reasons that I will explain later.

One night I was at Granny's house, Mum was there too. So, it was just the three of us and we decided that we were going to open up Nan's ashes that night. Granny went over to carry the box but she couldn't bring herself to open it. So, I took it upon myself and offered to do it. And as soon as I looked inside, I couldn't move, all I could do was stare inside the container. It was really difficult to comprehend that the contents of this box in my hand were the remains of one of the most amazing woman that I knew.

I heard Mum come back from the kitchen with a teaspoon and that brought me out of my dreamlike state. Using the spoon, we started to fill our miniature urns. Once we had filled our urns, we then decided to fill up a seal-tight jar with some of Nan's ashes. Into that jar went in 18 scoops of her ashes, one scoop for every year that she lived in Redhill. Mum, Granny and I took it in turns to fill up the jar. The reason why we did that was because those ashes that went into the jar were going to go into the River Thames, as that is where our great grandad's ashes were scattered. We didn't know when we were going to put them there, all we knew in that moment was that's where we wanted them to go.

I couldn't believe how much was still left inside the container, having never experienced this before. It was those remaining ashes that went into the church memorial garden. We just needed to sort out a date that would be suitable for all the family to attend, especially as my brother is away half the time, so we needed to work out a date where he would be home.

Chapter 18
A Rose for Each Generation

January 22nd 2017: it was the day that we had to lay Nan's ashes. The day before, Neil and Jake went down to the church grounds and dug up the plot where Nan's ashes were to be laid. Walking up to the church, I saw the plot. My eyes instantly welled up, but I managed to hold it together.

I had four white roses in my hand. They had to be white as that was Nan's favourite colour rose. The reason as to why I only had four was because it meant that Mum, Granny, Jake and I could all lay down a rose, symbolising the four generations.

As we were getting nearer to the church, out of the corner of my eye I saw a woman. This woman that I saw, she had a bad reputation of snooping around the church memorial garden and stealing flowers from there, flowers that had been laid down by relatives or friends in memory of the deceased that have their ashes in the memorial garden. I turned my head fully to face her. I held up the flowers so she could see them and gave her a look that said "I dare you," turned my head back around and walked into the church with my family.

After the church service had finished, we all went outside and headed over to Nan's plot. Jake carried the ashes over and the church vicar said some lovely words. Whilst the vicar was speaking, I was trying to separate the bunch of roses without making too much noise. One of the ladies from the church had the audacity to tell me not to separate them. I soon put her in her place and after that she didn't say another word – the cheek of some people these days is unreal.

After the Vicar had finished speaking, he asked Jake if he was okay to pour Nan's ashes into the ground, giving him the option that if Jake felt like he couldn't go through with it, then he would take over. Jake said that he would do it and I was so proud of him.

Once Nan's ashes were poured, we covered the plot with soil, then Granny placed the plaque in the ground. After the plaque was placed, I handed out the four roses. I gave one to Granny, one to Mum, one to Jake, and I kept one. We each took it in turns to lay the roses around Nan's plot. Granny went first, Mum went second, I went third and Jake went fourth. It had to be that order because that's the order we were all born: Granny had Mum, Mum had me first and then Jake second. We placed the roses around Nan in a diamond shape. We all stayed a moment before making our way home. As we walked away after saying goodbye, I had this really horrible feeling that all four roses wouldn't be there the next day. I don't know why I thought that, I just felt like something bad would happen to those flowers. I almost didn't want to leave for that reason.

I went down the following day and I was right. One rose had been stolen from my Nan. Originally there were four roses. I was now staring down at three. I had a good idea of who took it and instant anger took over me, to the point where I was shaking. I rang Granny and I asked what number this woman lived at. When Granny asked me why I needed to know, I explained what had happened. Once I hung up the phone, I made my way over to this woman's house.

When I got to her house, I knocked on the door but I got no answer. The second time I knocked a little louder to which I still got no answer, and the third time I knocked so hard I thought I broke it, but I got an answer, so it worked. Her husband answered the door and I politely introduced myself to him and explained what had happened. "Hi, my name is Rianna. Can I please talk to your wife about my Nan's ashes? They were laid in the church garden yesterday and one of the four roses that we laid has gone missing. I know she walks your dogs every morning and she goes past the church, so I would like to know if she knows anything about it." He was quite co-operative and didn't argue with me. He politely went and got his wife.

Eventually she turned up and I was now face-to-face with the woman that I suspected took the rose. I started off by saying, "When you walked your dogs this morning, you may have noticed the new roses that were placed down in the church garden, the white roses. They were my Nan's, she had her ashes placed there yesterday and one of them is missing. Do you know anything about that? I'm not accusing you, but you do have a reputation of being near that garden when you shouldn't be." She became quite fidgety. She couldn't look me in the eye, so I knew she had something to do with it but without visual proof I couldn't accuse. She was taking too long to answer for my liking, so I repeatedly asked her again if she had anything to do with it. "Did you have anything to do with it?" Of course she denied the whole thing, despite the fact that I knew she was lying directly to my face. I had no choice but to leave. I could feel the fire burning up inside me. I felt like a volcano before it was ready to erupt. I knew if I started to retaliate then I would get myself into a lot of trouble, which is something that I didn't want to deal with.

Just before I left the church car park, I went over to my Nan's plot and I made a promise to Nan that I would never let anyone touch her again. And still to this day since I stood up to this woman, nothing has gone missing from that garden. So I guess you could say that my suspicion was right as confronting her clearly worked.

Chapter 19
Another Year Older

Today is the 29th January 2017, my birthday. Now like most people, I usually get quite excited when it's my birthday but this year I didn't feel that bothered about it. It just felt like any other day. I wasn't really in the mood to celebrate it. Not like I would usually feel. This year it felt different. I had already made it clear to people that I didn't want to do anything big this year, just go out for a meal with my family, so that's what we did. However, before going out for dinner, I made a promise to myself that I would go down and see Nan.

I went to the shops to buy some flowers and then my friend drove me down, however, when we got there something was stopping me from getting out of the car, like a little voice inside my head saying to me, "Don't go over, you'll upset yourself," whilst another voice in my head was also saying to me, "Go on, lay the flowers down otherwise you'll regret it if you don't." A few moments went by and I made the decision to get out of the car a lay the flowers down.

I started to walk over to Nan's plot and when I got to there, I started talking to her, wishing she was here to wish me a happy birthday, just one last time. I started to think back to my birthday last year. I had the day off work. I like to take my birthday off every year. So, I went round to see Nan and as soon as I walked through the door, Nan gave me this smile that just lit the room. I walked over to her, gave her a massive cuddle and a kiss on the cheek. I told her I loved her, like I always used to do. And she patted me on the head like she always did and laughed. I remember asking her what day is it today and she pointed to a card that she had on the table with my name on it. It was a birthday card. So she knew. Either that, or it was just a lucky guess.

I was smiling a lot whilst I was thinking about my birthday last year but out of nowhere a car went zooming down the road so fast that it shattered my thoughts. I started to cry because I missed Nan. I looked at my phone and realised what the time was. I said to Zoe that we better make a move so I said my goodbyes to Nan and headed over to the car.

We just sat for a while before we actually left. I wanted to have a few moments to calm myself down first, I didn't want to walk into the restaurant with red eyes and a blotchy face from where the tears had been. Plus, I didn't see what the rush was. "You can't have a birthday meal without the birthday girl."

Chapter 20
Nan's Birthday

February 15th 2017: Today would have been Nan's 95th birthday. And it felt really weird not buying her a card or a present or anything, only a bunch of flowers to lay on her grave. I was very particular about the flowers that I chose. They had to be white roses as they were always her favourite. I know most people tend to like the traditional red roses but no, white roses are different, and I think maybe that's why Nan loved them.

As I made my way over to Nan, I started to think back to last year and what we did for her birthday. Mum and I went over to Nan's house, Granny was already there, Nan's cousin and an old family friend were there too which was lovely. As I mentioned earlier, last year for Nan's birthday, we watched the horseracing on the TV and we all put in a small amount of money before each race; like usual, Nan was the winner of the day.

Thinking about previous birthdays, I also remember how different Nan's 90th birthday was; this was her last birthday before she fell ill. Most of her family and friends were there as we had booked a hall for the event. We celebrated her 90th birthday at Reigate Manor Hotel. There we had a sit-down meal, plenty to drink, lots of laughs and just general chit-chat. Halfway through the day, Nan did a speech. I don't think Nan was ever really one for speaking in public as she kept it short and sweet. She just thanked everyone for turning up and making her 90th birthday one to certainly remember. I remember towards the end of the night – at this point I think it was fair to say that we'd all had a fair bit to drink as the waiters kept the wine flowing throughout the day – Nan's cousin and I were sitting in the reception area having a chat, talking about what a wonderful day it had been, and how lovely it was to get all the family together, and at one point in our conversation, she said to me, "Here, Rianna, do you think the hotel would notice if we took these chairs? I'm sure they can afford new ones if we took these."

I remember replying with something like, "It's not a question of if they can afford new chairs, it's more about how do we get them through the door and into a taxi without being noticed."

She said to me with a smile on her face, "Well, you'll need to find a way, because I don't think I can stand," and at this point I had lost it and was cracking up with laughter.

It's strange though, isn't it, looking back on everything, how one minute everything seems so perfect and then the next minute it's all changed. Just like that, in a blink of an eye, and everything is different.

Just one short year later for Nan's 91st birthday, I was giving Nan her birthday present to her whilst she was lying in hospital fighting to get better.

Chapter 21
Mothering Sunday

26th March 2017: Today is Mother's Day. Mother's Day was a difficult day for everyone, especially for Granny as she was the first descendant. The crown that Nan wore for all these years as the head of the family got passed down to Granny, and she is now the new queen of the family.

Every year for Mother's Day, not only would we buy cards for our Mum, but we'd buy one for Granny and for Nan. They too are mothers and it's sometimes easy to forget that. It's easy to buy a card for just your mum, but we need to include our grandmothers and great grandmothers, because if it wasn't for them, then there would be no us.

Without Nan, there would be no Granny, and without Granny, there would be no Mum, and without Mum, then Jake and I wouldn't be here. Today just didn't seem right not buying a card for Nan for Mother's Day.

I guess that's just part of adjusting to Nan not being here. Nothing will ever feel right on special occasions, when prior to now every year has been the same. It's like you get so used to doing something for so long that you find yourself getting into a routine. Once that routine changes, it's hard to get used to. It takes a bit of time to adjust to the new reality.

Chapter 22
Eleven Months an Angel

July 27th 2017: It has now been 11 months since Nan passed away and people say that you never get over a loss, which is certainly true. However, you do learn to live with it. You get up every day and go to work, you still go out have a laugh with your mates, but it's still somewhere in the back of your head. You even find yourself in a situation and wonder what would Nan do, would she want me to do this or say that, would she even want me to write this book? I hope so.

It's scary just how fast time flies. When Nan first passed away, I never thought that I would be able to cope without her. I couldn't see a future without her in it. But you do cope, one day at a time.

If someone told me this time last year that Nan wouldn't be here, how I would feel would be unimaginable. I would probably say something along the lines of "Shut up, you're lying, Nan's not going anywhere for a long time." Nan always had this saying which went "I'm not going anywhere as I've still got work to do down here."

At the time of Nan's passing, I was working as a care assistant in a care home for adults that have complex medical needs. I loved my job but at this moment, it became a chore. I was always angry, which affected my ability to focus on my job. I didn't feel like I had the support from my then manager at the time. Yeah there were a few staff members that were there for me, but it came across to me that my manager at the time didn't seem to give a rat's arse.

I made an appointment to see the doctor to ask for help, because I couldn't stop the recurring nightmares. If I had to describe the nightmare that kept replaying in my head night after night, it went as follows: It always began at the point that the undertakers walked into the room, watching them wrap my Nan's body up in the bed sheets, watching them gently place her on the stretcher and then taking out that horrible black body bag and placing it over her frail body. I watch them carry her out to the car and then watch as they place her body into the back and see them drive off. This is the point where I wake up and the memories of what happened all come back to life. These nightmares left me feeling angry all the time, to the point where I was hitting things, and I knew I needed help. I was very up and down and I didn't know how to control my emotions. I ended up needing counselling, which really did help me. It became a safe place, where I could just sit down, talk about everything, get mad, have a cry and I wouldn't be judged. Counselling is something that I never thought I would need, never thought I would even consider it as an option. I always saw it as a weakness to go and talk to someone. However, in reality, it's the total opposite. It takes a brave person to admit that they need help, to admit that they are struggling with their current situation and as a person that has been through it, I can now appreciate the benefits, and I am not ashamed to say that I needed help and would highly recommend it to others.

In total, I had six sessions of counselling, one-hour long session per week. Despite my weeks of counselling, my head was still a bit of a mess and to be honest, I think it will be for a very long time.

As my counselling programme went on, I came to realise one thing. What I realised about counselling is that it doesn't take the pain away and it doesn't make you forget what's happened. What is does do is train your mind to cope with your current situation in a healthy way.

Chapter 23
One Year Without You

Sunday 27th August 2017: Today marks the first anniversary of Nan's passing.

I woke up reasonably early for a Sunday. My family and I were going to go to church as that is where Nan is, a sign of respect to our little angel. The vicar read out Nan's name during the church service to mark the first year's passing. After the service was finished, we left pretty much straight away as we had to drive to Trowlock Island, Teddington.

It was a bit of a journey to get there, however the reason we went to Teddington is because we decided to place the rest of Nan's ashes that we kept behind, into the River Thames as that is where Nan put our great grandad's ashes. We separated these remaining ashes into four small jewellery boxes. Together, we all threw ashes into the river, each followed by a white rose which we all watched as the river carried it away. As a family we thought it would make a pleasant way to mark the one year. It was kind of our way to say to Nan, "We have coped for a year without you, and as a family we will continue to do so, so now's the time for you to be with Granddad."

As I said previously, we had coped as a family for the last year without Nan and now the time feels right for her to be reunited with the man that she loved, the man that she married at the tender age of 20, the man she built her life with.

We watched in silence until the roses had been carried out of sight by the gently flowing water. We took a slow walk up to the sailing club where Nan and Granddad belonged. We originally only went there to have a quiet drink for Nan, however something happened that we weren't expecting. There were members of the sailing club that knew Nan and Granddad, they had recognised Granny, so they came over and sat with us. When they asked why we were there, we then explained what had happened. Whilst they were talking, I spotted Nan's name on the wall. I got up and had a closer look. I said to myself, "The first woman to become rear commodore back in 1988, and then back in 1990, Nan became vice commodore." I looked at her name in awe, and I felt so proud to be her great granddaughter, that the name on the wall that I am looking it, that's my Nan.

I looked back over at the table where Granny and some of her old friends were sitting and it was a lovely sight to see. I smiled watching them having a drink. I went back over to the table. As I sat down, they were talking about old stories and I was just listening to them, laughing and hearing things about Nan that I didn't know, yet I thought I knew most things already.

A friend of mine told me a little saying which up until recently I had never heard of. It goes like this: "Knowledge is like a ball of wool in a box, you only know how much you already know, but you don't know how big the ball is as you haven't learnt it yet." It means that no one can ever know everything as there's always something new to learn inside the box.

After we had our drinks and said our goodbyes, we went out for a meal and had another drink for Nan, this time it was an alcoholic one, which was nice. We were talking about how the day went, and I think we were all pretty much thinking the same that actually, it couldn't have gone better. The weather certainly played its part in making it an appropriately lovely day for a beautiful lady, who still to this day and forever more, will be dearly missed by me, the rest of the family and everyone else that had the privilege to know her.

When I got home that evening, I reflected on the past year, thinking about how much things have changed from then up until now. Whilst I was thinking about everything, the title of this book came to my mind: "ONE YEAR WITHOUT YOU".

Dear readers, a personal message from me:

This concludes the story of how one single phone call changed my life, how as a family we coped with Nan's sudden illness and how I personally dealt with the first year of losing Nan.

Everyone deals with grief in their own way, there is no time limit on how long it takes, and if you want to know my opinion on grief, I feel that there is no right or wrong way to deal with it. To whoever is reading this, I want you to know that you are never alone, even in your darkest hour where you may feel like it.

If you have recently lost a loved one, or do so in the future, then I hope my words and experiences that I share with you, bring you some comfort in knowing that it is possible for time to heal a broken heart.

All my love,
Rianna. xxx